Darkness on the Face of the Deep

Darkness on the Face of the Deep

Poems by

Patrick T. Reardon

Cover design by Shay Culligan

ISBN: 978-1-954353-76-3

Kelsay Books
502 South 1040 East, A-119
American Fork, Utah, 84003

For Thomas Pace

and

Joan Servatius

and

Sarah, John, Tara, David, Emmaline, and, as always, Cathy.

~

Thank you, Thomas Pace, for suggesting this collection of poems.

Thank you, Haki Madhubuti, for friendship and inspiration.

Thank you, Bob Dylan, for more than half a century of poetry and for the line in "Spirit on the Water" which forms the title of this collection.

Thank you to the writers of the Bible, particularly Genesis in which the second verse is: "And the earth was without form, and void; and darkness was upon the face of the deep."

Acknowledgments

Thanks to the publications where these poems first appeared:

CC&D: "Front Porch"

Down in the Dirt: "Family Package"

eris & eros: "He Tossed His Sin Stone"

Esthetic Apostle: "Towers Loom"

La Piccioletta Barca: "Lamentations Road"

Meat for Tea: "It'll Get You There" and "Sambo"

Panoplyzine: "Robot Factory"

Poetry Quarterly: "Dust"

San Antonio Review: "After Reading 'State of Relax' by Eileen
   Myles" and "Communion of Saints"

Silver Birch Press: "How to Breathe"

Tipton Poetry Journal: "Itch"

UCity Review: "Goddess Dementia"

The Write Launch: "Angels Are Out Tonight," "City Hymn,"
   "Heron," and "Pa"

Contents

Manufactured the Earth

Constant Streetlight

Pa

Drive Chronicles Avenue straight out
of downtown for three miles to the
railroad bridge, empty as a Roman
ruin, turn right toward the spray-paint
chaos of the Grass Lake rocks, right
again onto Esther Road, to 135, and
there's tight-wound Pa sitting on the
dusk porch while nervous fireflies,
trespassers, skitter, knowing nothing
else, around the maypole of his chair.

From time to time, he slaps out with
a grimed 1940s gas station swatter,
and, when he connects, steps daintily on
the stunned creature with the sole of his
right boot, drags that sole toward him
along the porch wood, leaving, godlike,
quick-dying sparkle. We keep out of his way.

Stolid Ma encases herself in jobs to be
done as if rest is a gap in breathing.

Her grave is out on 12th Street, just east
of Mystic Boulevard, in the plot she shares
with Pa as she shared their bed of relief.

Pa died slowly, silently, from a wasting,
pale as smoke, fearful even more of death
than of life, with no caressing god to
provide welcome, just a blank white he'd
glimpse here and there, now and then,
and shudder, lock up inward. No escape.

Garden of Eden Groceries, the family firm,
still opens and closes each day, weekends
included, Christmas excepted. Pa ran a tight
ship, each an assigned post: sister, brother,
niece, nephew, in-law, cousin, crowd of
vague similar faces: Jane-Joan-June-Jean,
Garry-Larry-Gerry-Joe. Everyone's head turned.

Ma wanted me out of there, oldest and
a girl. Pa had an eye. I was the one sent
out from the store each day to travel up
and down Babylon City, buying what we
needed, arranging deliveries to Holy Galilee
Hospital, the Tyre County Department of
Corrections and City Hall where Pa knew
a guy in the Sewer Department who gave
a filing job to Leah, a year younger than
me—Ma's idea again—which Pa used for
inside information about street work, bids
and free bricks until, after Pa and Ma were
dead and gone, she quit and took the same
job for a lawyer across the street on the
6th floor of Maccabees Tower and hated
it just as much until one noon, while I was
sitting on the bank of the Babylon River
seven blocks away, she took herself up
to the roof and jumped her freedom flight
of wonder-filled license to the downtown
pavement in front of three teenagers
from west suburban El Dorado.

"Lot of good it did her," said Father
George, the youngest of the boys, a John
Paul II priest, quickly shushed by the sisters
who knew proper etiquette. No pedophile,
he—too empty for lust. I slapped him.

Now, evenings, if you drive to Esther
Road, you'll find me on the dusk porch in
Pa's old chair. I leave the lightning bugs
alone. Leah whispers in my ear, but I can't
burn the house down. Where would I live?
It is the last Sunday of Ordinary Time.

Robot Factory

Windows broken, robot
factory silent, acres of
weed-written empty—
I flame by on Cain & Abel
Highway for Albuquerque,
wanting to get where I'm
going—a messiah boy
from the hills, quiet and
pleasant, who assures me
all will be well but comes
down with grim Covid. Ye
of little faith.

I wander the Old Town
at mid-week noon, low
humidity but hot enough
to saute my memories,
and, in the black blotch
my eyes see, I am
spelunking outside St.
Louis and come through
one more erratic birth
cave to find the still
moveless body of Jesus,
but it is only Saturday, so
I let him sleep, and come
out to daylight just feet
from cliff edge where I
rappel 100 feet to the
path below, look back up,
step back away, to realize
it is the old stone face of
solemn John of the Cross.

After breathing into a
brown bag and wiping off
what little sweat there is
on my forehead, I enter
the cool white-washed
nave of San Felipe de Neri
Church. I sit. Later, a
cassocked guy steps lively
up the aisle marble, full
of animal vim, to my pew:
"You're snoring."

"Bless you, too, Father, for
I have sinned." It's only a
few hot blocks to the heavy
A/C of McDonald's on Central
Avenue Northwest and a
free-refill Diet Coke, and a
table a few feet away from
a guy with sun-coffee-ed
skin and some sort of handgun
in his under-arm holster and
an anger against Bulgarians
and a woman so pale she
must be from up North, and
I'm getting the impression
that she is ready to doze
off and he used to work at
the robot factory until the
owners gutted it and shipped
away the machining machines
—to Bulgaria, I guess—

leaving him in the same lurch
I'm in, needing salvation of
any flavor but only finding a
sick kid, mild sunstroke and
a vexed man of God.

Lamentations Road

Lamentations Road runs past
Judge Westcott's mansion, out
to Weed Hollow where a dead
mule rots, a pestilence of flies,
while I rock in the sun, another
broken part of the machine.

The Adolphus Smythe County
courthouse sits like a giant
toad off Maine Street along
Dakota Highway (Route 77), at
one time the fastest way to San
Francisco from Boston through
prairie dust thunders and rolling
green boredom and snow logic.

    You know because
    you read the book.

Her blood soaked into the cracks of
sidewalk, jagged grass-stalk garden,
in front of Brady's Old Style as rigs
rhythmed past on Dakota, as the
constant streetlight gazed down
like an absent-minded deity.

One of her wigs was employed
to cover the hole, and an angry
nephew hid the gun in the foot of
the casket, slid into the flames;
bullets exploded; Mike Shannon of
Shannon and Sons Funerals was
unctuous in his unsaid fury.

The box held her ashes and the
twisted metal of the gun and the
cracked, warped rods that had
held her back together through
much of sixty-four years; sent FedEx
to her son in Alaska, set off alarums;
NSA sifted through her grit and
relics for another bomb.

    Tattooed bones
    under skin.

I hate Judge Westcott's want of
question, Mike Shannon's soft palms,
Brady behind his joke, that wan,
bewildered boy for fleeing to
Alaska when he had the chance.

My diary was found in the flood three
springs after I had uncomposed my
poem on that midnight sidewalk, and
the stolid second-grade boy hid it, a
private scripture, in the crawlspace,
even though he was spanked for getting
muddy, twice. He learned a lesson.

    Waltz, baby, waltz.
    Music the Lord's echoes.

An over-muscled garbage truck, with
clumsy speed, bumps through the
Weed Hollow potholes and heads to
the McDonald's on Colossians Street
where it's Big Macs for all, including
the earbud yellowvest sitting alone,
eyes 1,000 miles away, mouthing the
revival lyrics of "Running Down the
Halls of Heaven" by The Humbled
Ones. He went to a special school.

After Reading "State of Relax" by Eileen Myles

Calliope of poem,
lustful, subtle—
nation un-uniting itself
and sighing,
postcoital.

"Cows kissing goats"
—Bible-immersed, I see
lions bedding with lambs.

Nebraska as
"the loosest kook of all and
animals walk naked in your past."

All the naked animals,
all the naked flowers,
all the naked stones and water bodies.
My nakedness.

My mother constantly enlists me,
oldest of many acolytes,
to rearrange her furniture,
empty of life now 25 years.

Bas Jan Ader,
70s performance artist, performing
in small boat on rough water,
"his toes leaning
over the edges of Provincetown"
and disappearing. Here, and
appearing/disappearing in
Linda Nochlin's *Bathers,*
Bodies, Beauty with
Courbet's *Origin of*

the World and
Alice Neel by Alice
Neel and *The Escape of
Rochefort* by Manet and Sam
Taylor-Wood's *Fuck, Suck, Spank,
Wank.*

Myles ran 30 years ago for president,
openly female.
They might just as well have tried
openly human.

Just a thought.

And Myles was poemed
by Zoe Leonard: "I want a president,"
which starts:
"I want a dyke for president."

And a president
who didn't have air conditioning,
who'd eaten hospital food,
who'd had an abortion,

and Leonard
didn't know why
the nation's chief executive
had to be "always
a john and never
a hooker."

My crowded childhood,
shorn of odd angles
and wearing an asylum jacket,
like the other many altar servers.

The cavorting states and commonwealths
—a state of play—
of the messy, slippery, punch-drunk,
grit-scratched Myles fever-dream
of the Un-united States
—Oregon sleeping in the arms of Washington—
are the baby me,
the one who dodged
the blanket of imperative,
the collar of big boy,
the bassinette constraint
—"Georgia on an eating binge"—
not me, not the one here.

My
bones ache to flee.

My
skin is electric lust for aloneness.
Call it crowdliness.

Told ugly, I stride,
grabbed as I am
by hands on
knee, elbow, nose, ear, cock, buttocks.

Joan of Arc died in flames, and, 30
years ago, Myles poemed her listening to
legends, hearing voices in

bells, and leading Charles VII to
throne, and, at 19, while still
living, she was burned at the
stake and, dying, "a dove leaped
right out of her mouth."

Right out.

Things Myles failed to note:
(a) Charles VII abandoned Joan.
(b) Susanna's Elders stood close by to
watch the blaze strip the girl to her
skin so they could be sure she was
a girl.

Openly human.

Never had a period.

I yearn the consolation of Washington.
I itch to be a loose kook.

But relaxation is death.
Always furniture to move.

*Note: The three poems referenced here are "State of Relax" by Eileen Myles,
which appeared November 3, 2020, in Art Agenda at https://www.art-
agenda.com/features/359179/state-of-relax; "I want a president" by   Zoe
Leonard, written in 1992 and available at LTTR athttp://www.lttr.org/journal/5/i-
want-a-president; and "Joan" by Myles, published in 1982 and available in an
audio version at poets.org at https://poets.org/poem/joan-audio-only.*

Call Me

Call me night of betrayal,
dark angel visit, mechanized mourning.
Keep the line moving.

Call me cancer on the back undiscovered.
Call me thunder of the poor.
Call me flowering sidewalk,
sharp-edge wood, whispering,
stone glass, funereal architecture,
spirits on the coin, spirit of stone.

Call me moon dog.
Call me beloved son,
wisdom, age and grace.
Call me amber waves of grain.
Call me street music lament.
Keep holy.

Call me Bull Run, Fort Dearborn, Agincourt.
Call me the life and strange adventures,
the fortunes and misfortunes of the famous.

Call me Interstate dromedaries
and middle-manager cherubim.
Call me all anthems, all lullabies,
all sagas and Iliads, all Great White Whales,
scratches, gnashings, itches.
Keep in tune. For God's sake, keep singing.

Call me irresponsible.
Call me maybe.
Call me on the line.
Call me on and on.
Keep your hands.

Call me gates of hell, plains of Abraham,
face of the earth.

Call me travels into several remote nations,
virtue rewarded, the life and opinions.
Call me Loop trudge, double spank,
echo of buckle on pew at Christmas.

Call me fathers on the sea,
at sewing machine haven,
on the bricked beat, blue as solid,
in the lonely pew, Our Lady of Sorrows,
the locked jaw.

Call me Mother may I.

Call me sun, moon, atoms,
sunlight shaft dust.
Call me weary lactation rooms,
frigid produce storeroom, heft fabric,
weight caress, blind sin eater.
Keep your nose.

Call me dark heaven, somber saints,
flame-tongue shadows,
sorrowed heroes of someone else's epics.
In the trauma that never ends,
sing holy pain, sacred ache.

Call me when.
Call me anything you want.
Call me, baby.
Keep the Lord's.

Call me empty artillery,
angry screaming-Mimis.
Call me lidded brain, bottled blood,
leashed electricity.
Call me steel and hard cotton,
broken bottle flesh, savor of soil,
blooded cement, red concrete,
hosing the freezings,
metal in the snow.

Call me Timmy.
Call me Al.
Call me Paw.
Call me tonight.
Call me a Sauganash, a wigwam,
a teared trail,
rambling Wolf sign, wordless,
snow rain, the fall of snow rain.
Keep faith.

Call me modern Prometheus,
tales of my landlord, posthumous papers.
Call me visions, flash dreams,
hallucinations, memoirs, blind whites,
transfigurations, recollections,
relic-ed flesh, horse-knocked inspirations,
ignorant sun, empty moon, pin-hole stars,
light from light.

Call me morning deceptions,
rigid columns of random motions,
archangeled blossom, mountained prayer,
chant—chant—chant,
daily office of eternal wrinkle,

spirit of oil, ice spirit,
incensed oil, sharp-edge wind,
sharp-edge fire, pigeon of hope,
water flow over closed eyes,
tongue of truth. Listen.

Call me lost tribes.
Call me communion of saints.
Call me pray, how, puzzle.

Call me windowed brick,
widowed search, tunnel light, surrender.
Keep quiet.
Keep peace.
Keep call me.

Family Package

I left my phone
on the back seat of a taxi,
and, when I borrowed one
from a cornrowed woman, gap-toothed,
the voice answering was
my dead Mother telling me
it served me right.

It was just a mistake, I said.

Your fault, she said from her ashes.
You were wrong.
You hurt your Father and me.
When will you learn?

I learned my lesson,
so did we all,
especially my brother,
until he'd had enough of lessons
and lessoned himself at his back door
in the snow rain of a 3 a.m. Saturday.

He called me from his ashes on my new phone
to say I was lost.

Yeah, I know.
I want you to find me, wherever you are,
but I don't know the address.

I wanted him to see me that night
when I am in left field
in the high school yard
as the dusk deepens to dark,

running away from the plate,
my arms out fully,
my eyes awkwardly to the sky,
my fingers reaching,
the ball never arriving.

My brother and I,
cassocked, surplice boys bowing
for the Prayers at the Foot of the Altar,
fake Latin syllables we don't understand.

I left the book of my life
on the back seat of a taxi
where a girl of six found it
and, unable to read the handwriting,
made it the Bible of her bookshelf,
the sacred mystery,
bleak and weighty in its chaos,
a formula beyond all divining.

Sambo

I delight
in book's side-by-side drawings
that 1852 physiognomist said proved
hairy hound terrier and hairy hound Irishman
were essentially the same creature,
two years after zoologist asserted
calibrations proved Negro equals ape,

and delight
to be far distant from that day and
from Patrick Riordan (Old Country spelling) who
starved, creature that he was, in the Famine
as the English dithered, debated, ate comfortably,

and delight
to enjoy my clear-eyed modern enlightenment.

>By the rivers of Georgia, we sat and wept,
>and our captors demanded a song—"Sing us
>so we have delight"—but how can we
>sing our song of Africa in a strange land?

I delighted
in my smiling baker grandmother,
full warmth and flour and flakey cookies,
who taught me—eeny, meeny—an evil nursery rhyme,

and in the poetry of my childhood in which
tigers raced in a circle and turned into butter
for the pancakes of Little Black Sambo who was me
(but, I knew, not me, dark and simple),

and in Fred Astaire and Judy Garland
minstrelling in blackface, so much fun,
and Bing Crosby, Frank Sinatra, Sophie Tucker,
Sophia Loren, James Cagney, Jimmy Stewart,
Dean Martin, Bob Hope, Douglas Fairbanks
and America's Little Darling, Shirley Temple,
as happy-go-lucky darkies—wasn't they a hoot!

By the rivers.

Table of Sinners

Roger Stone and Steve Bannon,
Donald Trump and I, at a lonely four-top,
far from the empty tables for the better sorts.
Don't tell me I don't belong.
No one in my family, none of my friends,
would tell you I am without fault.
Taint is taint. Even Job was tainted.
Our wretched company, communion of saints.

These guys commit whopping public sins
to fit their whopping chasms.
Mine are meek violations
to fit my meek ambitions, insect-like,
compared to their King-Kong transgressions—
Look at me! Look at me! Look at me! Leave me alone.

Proclaimed or secret, our sins weigh the same,
ego-ed as they are.
Who cares the size of the swimming pool turd?
For shame, such an inelegant image.

I am little, as they are little for all their bigness,
each tiny, lost,
whether with King-Kong or insect appetites,
measly, prodigals of pride and circumstances.
The baby's sorrows.

Have mercy on us.
We sit together, stewing each
in his lightless tunnels, caves, chasms,
a spelunker's dream,
journey to the tender center.

We dine on the same bitter eucharist.
Here, at this table of sinners, we are.
Sit down, you're rocking the boat.

Communion of Saints

Under the red Christmas tree,
she arranges a communion of saints.

In the DMV line,
a communion of saints: two teenagers in love.

A communion of saints,
electric with purpose,
heads for lunch
on noon Michigan Avenue sidewalks.

Through his Vietnam memories
float awkwardly a communion of saints.

After Lane Tech football, in the parking lot,
a communion of saints
—jammed in the CTA subway car,
in the Aldi's line,
living among the lost tribes,
strung out along the marathon route,
in the Graceland tomb,
applauding at the ballet,
in cardboard walls along Lower Wacker Drive,
blinded by moonlight,
found in the flood,
on a conference call,
after the whirlwind,
in the camp.

Read this list of those laid-off:
a communion
of saints.

Shouldering each other, hipping, angling,
a chaos of reporters clot
a communion of saints
for the sound bite.
It's a job.

Stiff, thick and distant,
a communion of saints lines
the morning-glint basilica cupola.

    The haloed birdman of Assisi:
    "I am the greatest sinner."

    Avila's haloed, Bernini-ed ecstatic,
    she too.

    Lisieux's little flower knew her guilt,
    though haloed.

    Peter's wrong,
    cock-crowed thrice.

    Communion of sinners.

On the long Oak Street beach sand,
in thick afternoon heat,
the bare sweat-sheen skin of a communion of saints.

In the jury pool at 26th and California,
a communion of saints fidgets.

All those people on your reliable wireless network
structure a communion of saints.

In his dust bannered-basement,
a communion of saints,
watching alone the Bears.

At State and Lake,
a rush-hour communion of saints
hustles up and down elevated station stairs.

My sweet, wounded brother
voted his guilt with his gun.

He marked his ballot
with a bullet hole and his pure blood
on backyard rain-snow grass and cement.

The White Sox roster, a communion of saints—

everyone in the Chicago City Council,
everyone on United Flight 5253 from Albuquerque,
all of the New Trier students moving between classes,

each person who stops
at Gallery 238 in the Art Institute of Chicago,
to puzzle the terra cotta *Adoration of the Christ Child,*
created five hundred years ago
by the workshop of Andrea della Robbia,
soft and delicate as grief,

all of us rising in this therapy elevator at 30 N. Michigan,
everyone who finds out today test results,
every baby born at Northwestern Memorial Hospital,
and golfer at Columbus Park,
and everyone trying on an awkward prom dress,
and sleeping baby,

and cop bending bulkily out of the squad,
and communicant,
and inmate,
Trump and Clinton,
everyone cumbersome with fear,
nun and hit man,
water and wine,
everyone numb,
everyone singing "Twist and Shout,"
everyone singing "I and I,"
everyone singing "Howl,"
every cheering voice,

and everyone, frayed and serene,
in blue-gold Alden Family Reunion t-shirts
in the Thaddeus S. "Ted" Lechowicz Woods picnic grove,
in the Cook County forest preserve,
off Central, near Elston.

    List (partial) of those born innocent—
    Hitler, Manson, Vlad, serial killers,
    Wilkes Booth, Pol Pot, genociders,
    torturers, Nero, Torquemada, enslavers,
    Ivan, Roy Cohn, profiteers, Stalin......

A communion of saints swarms
the blond-bright wood frame out west, past Aurora,
transmuting into a 3,598-square-foot single-family
on Stonehaven Circle, list price: $510,000.

A communion of saints,
shot over the weekend.

Dan Ryan, bumper to bumper,
a communion of saints—
power-walking the mall circuit,
behind the counter at McDonald's,
on the river trail bike path,
smoking outside Emporium in 2 a.m. Wicker Park,
renting shoes at Waveland Bowl,
writing poems,
writing tickets,
over the moon,
waiting for the laundromat dryer to cycle,
feeling the urgency,
under the thumb,
under the wire,
under the weather,
all those breaking the bread.

In the law firm conference room,
a communion of saints
signs the divorce.

At the ward office meeting, a communion of saints
gets marching orders for precinct work.

This night, a communion of saints will suicide.

At the Thanksgiving table,
place cards set for a communion of saints.

Yellow-vest parking meter techs,
five-year-olds picking at Happy Meals,
the make-upped guy in Starbucks,
uncomfortable in the dress he knows looks good on him,
Streets and San guys bowling in Mount Greenwood,

every lost lamb,
every saved soul,
all kissing women—
a communion of saints—
us and them,
flesh and blood,
quick and dead,
moth and rust,
cowboys and Indians,
every alley-dweller,
each of us who stumbles,
the children of the children's children,
seventy times seven,
all nations of earth,
all small and great creatures.

The fourth grader dreams a communion of saints
as she melts crayons on the silver school radiator
away from Sister's watch.

Everyone coming warily, angrily, hurriedly,
out of anesthetic,
everyone in the Lyric Opera, even mute supernumeraries,
every newly hired garbage worker,
every frayed teacher,
a communion of saints—
all of us riding escalators
at the James R. Thompson Center,
all of us ignoring the beggar,
all of us on the reservation,
all of us reading *Song of Solomon,*
all of us reading the Song of Songs,
all of us singing "Song of Myself,"
each one of us under the gun,

each of us uncertain,
all of us yearning,
all of us aching,
all of us feeling the tock and the tick.

Towers Loom

Loop towers loom behind their
gleam, and I can take you to the
parking lot just off Dearborn
Street where the Mayor and
reporters went down into
unflooded freight tunnels
(although that lot is likely gone
now, 26 years later).

Alex and I drove south to north
from city border to city border
through alleys of Chicago, world
alley capital. I saw a garage sale
chair and came back later to buy.

If you walk under the Loop and
follow the tracks west down Lake
Street—the soldierly tromp of
steel frames to oblivion—you
follow my brother's walk as a
twelve-year-old through a Sunday
summer afternoon (through black
hot neighborhoods where young
men and old, grandmothers and
skip-ropers saw him as a gray
-dungareed shaman, magic blond
boy), up back stairs, to the
Leamington second floor, 52
years before self-murder.

Younger, he and I crawled
around the new-poured
foundation of a Washington
Boulevard building, so muddy

and our bikes, we had to walk
them home to the double-
spanking for the double of us
by Dad, on the porch, then
after the bath in bed.

Up Western from 79th Street, I
drove to Chicago (800 north)
and turned left, out to the
reporter job in Austin. A
right turn, and, in a mile,
Ashland, where, thirty
years later, I walked with
Sandra the grit Chicago that
abraded her out to the
southwest and Mexico and
back southwest again, talking
of the dust on medical
implements in the drug store
window, dowdy Rexall, and,
a decade later, my son and
his wife live there in a duplex
with two fireplaces and never
saw the Rexall, gone now.
They can walk to work in
the Loop in looming towers.

Foreign Warning, Love Text

He Tossed His Sin Stone

He tossed his sin stone into Lake Deuteronomy,
set fire to his crops
and headed for Egypt City.

He divorced his ring finger with an axe,
slew his cattle where they stood
and set off down Galatians Road.

He gave up on soil,
wore ash sack cloth
and aimed for Pharaoh's gold.

He drank Red Sea thunder in the sun,
dined on lightning strike
and stormed up the two-lane blacktop.

He greased his hair with pig fat,
embraced Job's whirlwind
and stepped beardless toward Delta.

He cleared his mind,
emptied his bowels
and fasted for expected banquet.

He buried the saint upside down,
pilgrimed his strides
and visioned sanctuary.

He turned to arrival.
He conjured arrival.
He has yet to arrive.

Goddess Dementia

Goddess Dementia, come, waltz with me
down gray floors,
along sour green walls,
through Muzak air.

Undress me in my doorless room.
One button at a time, unfasten my pajama top,
unbutton the crotch of my bottoms.
Slip the blue and white stripes
off my purple-marbled legs
with your prying fingers.

Come, waltz with me.

On cool sheets, I squirt an arc of urine in the air,
my eyes on your eyes.
Your babe. Let us cuddle.

I mouth your plump nipple, suckle.
You run cool hands along my thin blotched skin
as if to flood me with blood. I faint.

Come, waltz with me.

You mount me like an angel, like a dancer, like a church.
Your dark hair storms.
My eyes on your eyes.
You smell of soil.

You proffer me a vision in your grotto,
Queen of the Universe,
Queen of Victory,
Lady of Sorrows.

You whisper in my ear a secret.
You whisper in my ear good-bye.

Come, let us waltz.

Lots Drawn to Inspect Stuffed Animals during the Class Visit to the Central Illinois Natural History Museum, Tuesday, March 27, 1923

Loser, he got
the skunk (which
didn't smell), but,
until school end,
his name was Fart.

Not a story to
tell biographers
when, after his
election, they
quick-stopped in
Decatur for a few
bricks to make
a first chapter.

In fact, none of the
boys, now men,
recalled much if
anything about the
oddly quiet kid, who,
that warm winter,
moved in and moved
away come summer,
except his side-eye
stare, and how do you
make that into a tale to
entrance a life-writer?

Later, out of office,
nearly out of time,
in his wheelchair,
pretty much blind,
he would rub his
fingertips along the
shiny metal frame
and see the glisten
of black-white fur,
not recalling the
museum moment
when he held the
stuffed carcass and
knew (for the first
time) he would die.

Drive

I picked up St Judas out
on Ecclesiastes Road,
hitching a ride to any place—
exactly where I was headed.
"I'm running out of gas," I
told him. "Drive," he said,
and I did, all that winter
and never stopped at a
pump. I slept in the front
seat. He slept in the trunk.
From his briefcase of dry
leather, he took a Rorschach
card for me to read. He said
it explained the rock wall
off the sorrowful desert
and the ghosts in the stone.
I didn't know what to say.
"Drive," he said, so I did.
We ended up on Proverb Street.
The bank was empty, and
the dress store. The cafe
only open on Saturdays. On
the steps of the courthouse,
an Oakie shouted at the
Mayor, "Help a starving man."
The Mayor had him arrested.
St Judas pulled me to the
statue of a dog that once
saved a family of twelve
from a burning dime store.
One of his ears was broken,
and I looked in the deep dark
of that bronze cave for a
road to modest paradise.

African Lion

for Haki Madhubuti

The lion of Africa, now
in winter, still burning bright.

Flame conflagrates still
those who have ears
to hear, raw hearts,
transmutes, transmits
vision—steel spine,
mother touch—as when
he first taught: Don't cry,
scream.

Ashes will come, but,
for now, for long
past, the fire of
wonder-rage-hope
roaring. Pride leader,
pride servant,
strength given, taken.
Let my people
Black.

A life on borrowed time—
street-death dodged.
A life stolen by artists—
lured into poem,
a whirlwind blossom.

Crack open pain.
Do what must be.
Do what can be.
Raw Black beauty.
The mighty Wall.

Do. Run at fear with
open eyes. Endless
fight till end. Endless
flame till out. Do. Ashes
will come. Now, blaze
your joyful Blackness.
Blaze!

Prairie Melancholy

In police-strobe darkness, steel-flesh-glass contortion
sculpted on the shoulder of Ecclesiastes Road,
velocity relic—two crosses now, names I never met.
Lay my burdens down.

Tall grasses sway
like slow hot dancers to inexorable song.

The Cosmos tick: the blossom in sun, soon under snow,
mundane massacre of yearning.

> Lapis lazuli, blue astonishment anguish,
> in the painting of the saint of the wealthy,
> as lost as any of us,
> as caught in siren comfort/brother pain,
> as raw as slash on forearm skin, blood smearing
> in angel wrestle at ladder foot,
> dolorous messenger with nothing to say,
> dislocated hip.

Swoop-swoop-swoop, night traffic
past the names, limp ribbons, faded pink plastic,
on to Omaha where, in a sticky gas station store,
the neck-flame clerk glares as if I want to grab
seven jumbo Cheeto bags, hug them to my chest,
escape.

> Carved into the roof of the sky, words
> of sacred wind spinning since the world
> began and, in the whirl, listen: the howl and
> a baby's insistent cry.

Into the hole, back, away from road edge,
back in dark, behind the two ribboned names, I
shovel a mound of crushed Cheetos, my road
map, thirty silver pieces, McDonald's brown
napkins, an ocean of worn Jewish shoes, a single
Marlboro, my brother's gun, an envelope of Tower
dust, a new translation of the Book of Job, my
burdens, my spit in the mud, and a bag of lost-tribe
action figures—soundless keening, amid the click of
blood, sap and Big Bang debris.

The Wheat of My Days

The wheat of my days is sown with weeds.
The wind does it
and the run-off from the hills
and, maybe, enemies.
  Who doesn't have enemies?

In my bread loaf, I
find scatters of green pulp.

I ingest pigweed and milk thistle,
bindweed, burdock and lambsquarters,
sorrel and St. John's wort,
yellow nutsedge, ragweed and knotweed,
Bermuda grass and wild carrot,
leafy spurge.

My unecstasyed visions are
infested with lusty stoats.
Cockroaches stride the
halls of my mind.
Mice hide in closets of
my memory
with termites, ferrets and
emperor rats.
Bed bugs and centurion
mosquitoes draw
obscene tattoos across my skin.

My correspondence is clotted
with dispatches from plague spots,
war scenes and natural disasters.

The angel of death
swoops through the house
a click before the A/C kicks in.

The city flag flaps forlornly in rain,
empty of glory.

Out on Highway 1, every few miles,
ribbon/plastic/laminate
shrines,
inelegant mourning
hymns,
some clumped at knife-edge turns,
dark places,
heavily shadowed in daylight,
where loss of
control waits
to spring onto the
laughing throat,
cartwheeling.

My small change falls on
the pew seat,
echoes wide and high,
the afternoon church vault void.

Silence follows, cool,
alive with
emptiness,
electric with
expectation,
ghosted by who sat here
yesterday
and in earlier years,

58

and back to the worker who,
after latching the wood leg
braces to the linoleum laid over
gray concrete,
rested here a
moment,
lost once again in an
afternoon doze
on a hill overlooking a
wind-waving wheat field
outside poor and
jolly Brindisi.

Great Amen!

Great Amen! Calliope elevated
train Loop-circuits and flings
out to Kimball, out to Harlem,
to Midway Airport, these souls
and those, bodies and smells,
viruses and conversations, and
brings others back, like blood,
like three-mile walk taken
every morning, constitutional,
like up and down basketball
court, until time expires.

Great Amen! Blare the horn.
Bray the trumpet. Announce
the fleet and lame, as we
board train, as we emerge
onto platform, as we spit
onto tracks, as we cough
into inner elbows, keep
our distance, crouch and
cower and back straight
our stance, as we board
train, as we strap-hang, as
we emerge and escalator to
street level where sirened
police car whoop-whoops
up State Street, as we join
the mufti communion of
saints rivering commercial
sidewalk, as we ride box
elevator with cherubim and
seraphim, as we submit to
tests by medical ministers

who feed us incantatory
words as a snack, as we
board train, as we window
cemetery stones and
ornaments below, Irish cross,
Eternal Silence, parallel
sphinxes, as we emerge,
as we are born onto
platform to go hither
and yon and back again,
as we board train, rewomb,
and keep together soul and
body, and ride through night,
sleeping in awkward warmth
unless rough wakened by cruel
Samaritan. God, bless the bum.

Great Amen! Exit at 79th, at
35th/Archer, at Annunciation,
at Cottage Grove, at Ridgeland,
at Noyes, at Pentecost, at
Ascension, at Deposition, at
Oakton-Skokie, sunbeam
through glass, at Sox/35th,
at Pulaski, at Purgatory,
whiter than light, at Cermak/
Chinatown, at K town, at
Uptown, at Boys Town, at
Bucktown, dawn over lake,
at Bronzeville, at Canaryville,
at Epiphany, at Hegewisch,
start of the line, end.

Great Amen! Urined corner,
chicken-bone bag rip, plastic
Fanta bottle rolling and back,
rolling and back, tock-tick of
Cosmos, eye screen, thumb
screen, alphabet screen, ear
buds, weight-shift with
acceleration, deceleration,
slight curve, wide curve,
sudden bloom of perfume,
smell of sweat, pondering
salt stains on Yankees cap
inches away, map to gold,
fatal X-ray, martyr signature,
foreign warning, love text.

Great Amen! Sunset light
beam blast forges, explodes
into wonder electric copper
curls under beret, woman
paperback-reading, cloud of
unknowing, moment for me
uncontainable, transfigured—
field of lilies, cloth of gold,
Solomon in all his glory—
then buildings, then bare
winter trees, then Wilson,
then she's up, out the door,
onto platform, and I now
have a place to sit.

Heron

Great blue heron, white in high green,
folds on self, forward falls toward water,
clear space, wingspan wind-catch, rise in flight.

I am semi-trailer truck in someone's tender canoe
—steep banks through suburbs, six crows
from one bank to the other frenzy a hawk,
mud raccoon handprints,
duckweed green scum.

I will never return to this river.

  Forty days and nights on
  rising waters, they alone
  kept the breath of life in
  their nostrils across the face
  of the seas. The raven, gone,
  and then the low pigeon,
  back, with green hope.

I write these words
on back of page proving evolution
equals original sin
—as if the heron were showing off,
as if God seeded evil,
as if Jesus was a mutation,
as if pain meant,
as if anyone could make me understand anything.

Here, twenty years after heron's fall,
bird, instruct me, odd, tall, thin, long creature.

Explain cell division, tock-tick and falling to fly,
neither evil nor good.

Bullets embedded in baby

Bullets embedded in baby,
capsuled in new-growth bone,
lodged against arteries, organs,
cased in sinews, fat, muscle.

Raised in home of shooters.

Stay, she said, in chair.
Eat, she said, meal.

Right arm not full-rotate.
Base of skull, sharp-spasmed.
Dull shock, electric ache.
Never unmetalled move.

Look, she said, elsewhere.
Trick, she said, mind.
Ignore.

Steel zygotes stillborn,
I carried them away
from home of shooters,

breast-clasped metal,
carried them, askew weights,
in stammer step, through stagger turn,

metal as me as skeleton and blood
and awkward thrusting yearn.

Ever above, around, under,
inert, alien,
as me as skeleton and blood—

reach, all is reaching.

Christening

Three airliners hang in late
afternoon air like ornaments
on an invisible tree, as tall
as the giant's beanstalk,
motionless at a few hundred
miles an hour, heading one-two-
three west from Lake Michigan
aiming along Irving Park Road to
O'Hare International Airport—
three small lights, 735 beings,
same bright, same size as
the single lamp over the parking
lot of Green Valley Grocery,

and there are many rivers to
cross, so here we go, I'll tell
you of the Queen Mother who,
on the 42nd day after giving birth,
whited-out the birth certificate,
blew on it, dried it, ran it through
her typewriter [as she had many
times before as Quaker Oats
secretary] and typed a new name,
christened a new curse, Whoreson,

and, sweating in weak A/C to
Joshua Street, showered, combed,
skitted, parked, folded out, avoided
dog turds in parkway, entered
courtyard of U-shaped building to
third doorway, to mosaic-floored
vestibule, Whoreson rang bell of
Lady East, buzzed in, upped stairs,
corridored to number and knocked,

and Lady East: "Forgot....busy
...," and Whoreson: "Sorry,"
turned [she was dressed for
dancing], corridored, downed,
to weak A/C, ashamed [knowing
she was dressed for dancing with
History Book whose ancestor, with
same bushy goatee, high forehead,
Cabineted for Lincoln, not knowing
how he knew, but he'd seen the
photo in the Lorant collection and
worked with History Book and Lady
East at the Bureau, saw their looks,
guilty for looking, ashamed to know],

and tongue flames roared over the heads of
Lady East and History Book and over
Saul the Boss and each being at desks,
on phones in the Bureau in gritty pentecost,
and over each being on Randolph Street,
even at 1 a.m. at shift end, and over
each being on the over-bright Ravenswood
el, communion of saints, lost tribes found,

and Whoreson stood with girl
when told to stand as the 7th grade
others watched, walked to the board
when told, and, on cleanest typed
lists where they ranked high, Whoreson
and girl drew lines with pens through
their names, sat when told, and, later,
girl, behind Whoreson in the empty
room, cried as before she had asked
in a whisper and he had told her,

and the steward squandered the
master's fortune, and the church
chant was clear: "Lift up curb rat,
sunflower tower, missionary hope,
half-carved marble, spilled wine,
brittle-leaf puddle, spittle, scream
in the night, wave wear, branch scar;
thumb-cross forehead, lips, chest,"

and Whoreson, 11, was punched on
the right cheek, buffeted, on the
Jackson Boulevard crowded bus by a
kid getting off: "Sorry," not knowing
what else to say, and Whoreson, 68,
dreamed of disappointing a Mexican
woman and, waking up, spent the day
saying "Sorry" to no one in particular,
and Whoreson, 25, kept a journal for a
year and, for the Joshua Street day,
mentioned nothing about Lady East,
typing several paragraphs about the
book just read and a fact armor of
this and that, mortared by "Sorry,"

and mountain gap, pilgrim crossing,
pitched tent, overnight embers, salt
the lamb, salt the stew, for strangers
on the border road, Sarah at tent flap
laughing, wait dawn, listen for horn
blast, plant mustard seed and journey;
thumb-cross forehead, lips, chest,

and, when Whoreson arrived at his
second job at Proverbs Athletic Club,
the phone message said the Lord had
called, jumped in the Pontiac, fleeing
to Moab, but the angel stood on 79th
Street with a flaming sword, so
Whoreson stayed, and, in time, was
ungrieved by the death of Queen Mother,
and ungrieved by the death of Totem
Father, but then his innocent brother
self-killed and Whoreson did not say
"Sorry," he listened to the electricity
that he and Whoreboy shared, and
grieved for the two of them,

and three airliners one-two-three,
now machine Santas with semi-truck sleighs,
growl over Irving Park Road toward
horizon, flames over the head of every
being in those planes, over the heads
of every walker, every driver on Irving,

and Whoreson sees in rear mirror
tongue of flames—or is it setting
sun?—atop his sweat-stained Yankees hat.
Thumb-cross forehead, lips, chest
and puzzle gospel.

Front Porch

5:30 sunlight, 5:30 shadows,
afternoon on mundane Paulina Street,
shadow-light layers,
on oak trees, lilac bushes, unmown grass,
Fords, Toyotas, Hondas, Chevrolets,
shadow-flecked red-brick wall, white-mortar-lined,
galaxies upon galaxies,
from 6220 to Granville Avenue,
cosmos of particles,
a robin che-upping a manifesto
about ownership, propagation,
extinction. Chicks to feed.

Siren over on Clark Street
forever approaching
until, finally, past and away.

Each bag of bones and blood, flesh and water,
cushions, cradles, clasps,
cuddles, contains, constrains
a newborn—
each rapid-Polish cellphoner
crouching to pick up his tiny dog's tiny shit,
each tall-sitting bicycle woman, goggled,
each radiant girl in flip-flops blushing into her phone,
each trucker and cop
and strollered-child and basketball-dribbler,
masked and unmasked,
each father, daughter, son,
each me
—each new born and yearning to find home
inside the electricity of muscle
and snap of thought
and unrelenting confusion of each day.

Breeze, almost cold.

Look at me on this porch here
in faded red t-shirt "Barnaby's,"
worth a buck-off at the pizza place in Niles.

I am, like any of you,
new born with every second's accident.

Itch

He reached out his
hand and I took
three steps upon
the sea and, then,
with the strong
wind, feared and
sank to the bottom
where I have been
ever since as stupid
armies with water-
logged firearms
clash in soundless
strife. The brochure
tells the story of
when truth and
knowledge met and
the still, silent itch
dug under my thick
skin. Thrones and
dominations fell
asleep at their angel
duty and the Son
escaped out a side
door to go bowling
with the blind
weightlifter and the
hip-hop doorman, a
radical trinity, if
there ever was one.
God bless the child.

Manufactured the Earth

Loss Leaders

Fled the courthouse for lonesome Mexico.
Fled flock-feeding, versed chapters, spiritual ringworm.

Fled through live soil fields, seeds risen to sway.

God from God, Light from Light,
I credo-ed, fleeing.

Fled the endless white, empty.
Fled womb's fruit in the sheen mirror.
Fled my unchild-ed childhood.
Fled Mary and Meg and Ken, dying.

> Translate
> breathing. Define
> voices in the
> shadowed alley.
> Explain tracks
> of blood and brain
> and touch of
> cement garbage
> box by the crab
> apple tree where
> David wanted to
> hide.

Fled galaxies and the recitation of Genesis in moon orbit.
Fled dust.

Fled down Chronicles Road.

Fled words carved in sky since the world began.
Fled human howl.
Fled death in the fetal position.

Be precise
about orgasm.
Spell the animal
hoot. Cackle.
Render the
weightless steps.
Construe a poem.
Pray in a line.
Draw a schema of
anxiety.

Fled the Nazarene and the Ishmaelite.
Fled war and whale and locked cell.
Fled angry woman and silent man, already old.
Fled Mary and Margaret and my brother who
will not come back no matter who gets asked.

Fled two boys unprepared for storm approaching.

Fled broken bread,
warm as in Grandma's kitchen
where she smiled—the sun
jeweling soil and dung and growing
things and creeping things and the newborn
and the dying and the dead,
her bread sprinkled with flour.

Fled demanded devotion.
Fled martyr and siren and electricity.
Fled furnace prophets, shouting but not their names.
Fled inhaled words.

Fled his somber bullet,
his ashes curb muck, roof
dust, grit in the hop-skip girl's
hair, wind-scattered.

I kept the breath of life in my nostrils forty
days and nights, the raven, gone, and then
the low pigeon, back, with green hope.

Fled fortress, bulwark, mortal ills,
foes, woes, power, flood, earth,
one grim word, strength, striving,
age, battle, acolyted altar.

Fled itch.
Fled back parts of elusive Word.
Fled thud in the night.
Fled whirlwind.
Fled the flaw of breathing.

Bright

The Bright Meadow subdivision, unbuilt,
except for the show house, boarded
up now against theft and further
calamity. The streets, there, a
crosshatch from the sky, gridded,
named by a blind-faith developer
who gambled that the Lord's book
would protect dear investment—

main intersection,
Deuteronomy Street and Matthew Way,
and, east-west,
Daniel, John and Luke Avenues,
and, north-south,
Numbers, Proverbs and Galatian Lanes.

Mornings, I abscond from the
mathematics of the well-ironed
American home that my parents
have walled up at the far edge of
Honey Hollow Acres and wander
those semi-sacred pavements amid
wilderness, amid weeds taller than
I am, and poke around that mournful
dreamhouse at 135 Proverbs Lane to
spot occasional damage from town
yahoos, young enough to splatter
the wood boards with "shit" and "fuck"
but not old enough to penetrate
this tent of tainted milk and dirt honey.

The unfinished land, for them, is a
nervous-making blankness. For me, an
earth scripture of mysteries more
consecrated than, in the old downtown,
careworn St. Thomas Aquinas, 110 years
old and counting, where, Sundays, we go
to add a check to Mother's list. Father
has nothing to say.

I walk every bald street in Bright
Meadow, east-west, north-south. Dust
on every thing, even weeds, fallen
incense, empty of aroma, but I know,
if I trace the right pattern on that dry
unborn streetscape, a gospel of joy will
open a fissure in the planet's crust that
I will dive into and never look back.

Bees make a hive in my skull. They
circle unstopping, electricking my
uncle's story of the Church of the
Tunnel, a niche in a redstone wall,
natural or not—inside, a level spot as
pedestal for the saint, Dominican-
gowned Teresa, three-quarters life-size,
un-ecstacied, foundress of Carmels
—inside, shoeless nuns and friars of this
wind-hewn desert where processions
come each year on the feast to the
wrinkle of rock beseeching salvation
or rain or forgiveness.

They Dated by Sidewalk

They dated by sidewalk,
masked, six feet apart.

She was tall,
long hair twined by wind and mask.

She was short,
all long dark eyebrows above mask.

From her height,
she could see clear line of center part,
pepper-salt roots
and, flashing, pre-plague purple-red curls.

From under eyebrows,
her eyes latched to each gesture,
each forehead line,
each reddening of cheek in cold.

Her skeleton,
long torso, long legs, delicate skull,
naked to electric gaze, charged.

Her warrior stomach stirred.

They dreamed,
innocent and shy in own beds,
of cotton swabs
and erogenous lips.

Hex

I wore the
hex as an
undershirt,
itchy every
second, led
to rashes
and grids of
scratch cuts,
wounds, led
her to yell
at me for
deep nail-
digging fabric
to innocent
flesh, though
she had her
own hex, a
limp with
every left
leg step that
she had
taught her-
self well to
unnotice.

I suffered
the hex. It
left the skin
of my face
pocked deep.
The flesh
was weak,
my spirit
bent in on

itself. She
yelled the
hex sores
bothered
her eyes.
I was
innocent
of answer.

I worked
the formula
forward and
back, but
each time the
answer was
hex, led her
to yell to
erase the
blackboard.

The hex lived
among the
lost tribes.
It had a seat
among the
communion
of saints. It
was the
shaman in
my tent, at
my camp
fire. She
yelled hex
was dirty.

I swallowed
hex at the
altar with
water and
wine, and it
poisoned
my blood
and bones.
At night, I
glowed like
radium or a
halo, never
knew which.
She yelled I
frightened
her, but I
was never
able to say
boo.

How to Breathe

Accept air in.
Process it. Expel it.

Accept bliss and ache,
random acts of existence.

Accept other voices
or don't listen.

Accept the flower and dog shit
or close your eyes.

Accept a journey
that starts and ends.

Accept the gamble
of waking up.

Accept limits.
Accept freedom.
Accept gravity.
Accept fragility.
Accept the cloud of unknowing.

Accept unscheduled beauty.

Accept your own sins.

Accept confused alarms,
bad intent,
the chafing of coupling.

Accept the communion of saints,
the quick and the dead,
the mob, the family, the dance.

Accept another's fingerprint.
Accept the risk of reaching.

Accept alone.

Accept the blinding white beyond.

City Hymn

Hymn the sewer line.
Hymn the rhythm.
Hymn mown grass,
dawn-sun broken glass,
ash tray brass,
my scar, the rusted-nail fall.

Hymn the sink hole.
Hymn girder.
Hymn cinder alley,
maggot alley,
the basketball-rimmed garage.
Hymn chaotic bloomed colors along the garbage fence.

The boy I am
studies in the concrete of my alley,
large smooth stones,
and seeks in their curves
answers to questions I don't know to ask,
my inhale-exhale.
Breath, breath, all is breath.

Hymn transaction, traction.
Hymn long division.
Hymn contrition.
Hymn lost and found,
the boy-brother seven-mile endurance
down the Lake Street el-track canal.
Hymn the crayons I melted
on the 5th grade radiator and
drew side views of Lincoln
as a conjurement.

Hymn the parquet floor, the open door,
the growl, the yowl, the pirouette, the give-and-go,
the vestibule mosaic, the bathroom tiles,
creosote planks, the silhouette Stations of the Cross,
butcher-shop six-point star.

Hymn sorting, shedding, shredding,
staying the course,
rubber-ball hockey in the snow alley,
computing my Lexon League batting average, .119.

Behind the Signboards facing Washington Boulevard,
tall weeds, mush cardboard, jagged glass bottles,
dogshit, a single discarded Playboy, charred——
impromptu boy battle, small rocks
into the weeds, out to the sidewalk,
one off my boy's forehead, a glance, a graze,
no matter, but,
turning toward older girls walking past,
a scream,
my sweat transubstantiated
to blood mapping my face,
Rivers of the World.

Hymn Leamington Avenue.
Hymn Granville Avenue.
Hymn Lindell Boulevard.
Hymn Mullholland Drive.

Hymn your own streets.
Hymn your own cities.

Hymn Saint Louis.
Hymn Chicago.
Hymn Calabasas.
Hymn Momence.

  The boy
  turns away
  from lines of children shoes and underwear
  on the family board,
  a numbers graph, an organizational chart,
  looks out
  to the curve of the earth,
  to the broken glass morning glint,
  to dogshit alleys,
  to street grid lines leading away,
  leading to puzzle and more puzzle.
  I breathe puzzlement.

  I am at the map
  and can follow West End east to the Loop
  or Maypole west to California, to China,
  to Russia, to Europe, to New York.
  I am on the map and fly
  to the edge of all that is
  and back to the Bang.

Hymn curb trash:
twigs, a leaf,
a mud-thick mitten from winter,
a rosary crucifix unlinked.

Hymn links and unlinking.
Hymn clouds of incense.
I will go to the altar.

Hymn clouds of leaf-burn smoke.
Hymn seedlings.

Hymn street cleaning.
Hymn no parking,
for sale,
loading zone,
no dumping.
Hymn don't walk.

Hymn electricity.
Hymn tree cover, plumbing, two-flats,
six-flats, courtyard buildings,
the bungalow belt, the forest preserve clearing,
lagoon scum, the dainty fox through tombstones.

Hymn the asphalt street.
Hymn the gum, black on sidewalk concrete.

Hymn the elevated,
the elevator,
the elementary school,
the exit ramp.
Hymn photosynthesis.
Hymn sun soaking the red-brick wall,
my untranslatable scripture,
the word at the start and the end.

Hitching Ecclesiastes

I saw David hitching out on Ecclesiastes Road
four years after the gun.

He was on the shoulder of the northbound lanes.
I was heading south.

His blond hair in back below the NY Giants cap
was black with thick dry blood.

He had a large sign, saying: "Going to hell."
He wasn't laughing.

He would have waved to me if he had seen me.
I'm sure.

Or maybe yelled and thrown the sign at me,
brotherly love.

Coming a year later, he was my crib twin,
screaming while I laid low.

The camera rises to a wide shot of the forest sunset,
foregrounding David and me.

My black car moves smoothly south down the ribbon road.
He stands alone in dusk.

The credits roll. His is a bit part.
Mine is played by a stunt double.

Can't Say Dallas

Behind the grassy knoll, they divide garments.
Behind Trinity Hill, they throw dice.

Can't say Dallas.
Can't say Dachau.
Can't say Hiroshima or Wounded Knee.

Sacred soaked soil.
Sacred pavement, shadowed wall.
Whisper rituals. Whisper contrails.   Remember.

Translate to music.

Can't say Matthew Shepard.
Can't say Chaney, Goodman, Schwerner.
Can't say Dutch girl's name.

Ben the barber transmuted the camp,
his life into nineties, six decades after and more,
breathed delicate elegy, voicing the voice-stolen.

Lee said: Don't cry, scream.
Lorde said: I am a fellow rider in the cattle cars.
The girl said: In spite of everything.

Dead bird, cacophony of feathers on the snow.
Once an anthem on the wing.

It'll Get You There

Follow 12 steps.
Chew sugarless gum.
Show up for counsel.

    Lines to stay within

Enjoy breathing.
Enjoy Diet Coke.
Take medicine on time.

    Answer when asked.

No need to understand.
Check off boxes.
Listen to instructions.

    Avoid those thoughts.

Only get in the car to go somewhere.
Walk briskly past the gun store.
Do not search the internet for guidance.

    Dead brother's blood.

Before you encapsulated the scream,
you were wild with agony.
So were the others.

    The others.

Doubly agonize them?
Doubly rend their skin, break their bones?
Doubly self-empty?

Do no harm.

It'll form the frame to fit your portrait.
It'll get you there.
It'll swaddle.

Urgent

Breathe.
Stay.
Live.

The Book of JoJo

In my solitary
dormitory with a
whore in every
mirror, I shaved
off my beard and
shaved my head
and shaved my
eyebrows, oiled
my skull with
balsam and myrrh
and took the call
from my brother
who sang "Old
McDonald" as I
planned suicide.

And I saw two
police run into
flame building
to bang doors,
and the overcome
fireman fall through
floor after floor to
become hero of
story told over and
again to two small
boys on their way
to nuns like geese
in full flight.

And I heard sin
songs and turned
away and turned

away and turned
away, sinful
enough already.

And I read, in
the Book of JoJo,
of rich man turd-
hilled, his coin
stolen, his people
erased, his skin
boil-rupted, and
he complained
to Unseen,
and Unseen
whirlwinded him,
bullied him, awed
him, to humility
and surrender, or
anger and surrender,
either way surrender
since what else?

And I gnawed
cottonweed and
thistle bottom,
einkorn, emmer
and spelt, festuca,
rye, forb, wort,
nutsedge, St. Louis
ivy, creeping clover,
pitch and chaff.

And I sweated in
thick weave jacket,
at the banquet
where sweated
dancers circled and
I fingered behind
my back brocade
wallpaper, could
feel the red, and
knew I was not
understanding.

And I saw fierce
frail woman, a few
steps from dust,
bully feeble
docile man to
McDonald's table,
to eat Egg McMuffin,
while counting coins
and calculating,
bent with one
thousand months,
stooping to tie his
shoe, his flesh
dry as yellow grass
in a dirt city where
rain is long ago and
lush lot is brittle,
withered as his leg,
sored, mottled flesh
that, once, she
stooped to lick
of salt and sweat.

And I heard Gabriel's
trumpet over the
downtown crowds,
over the lone subway
woman with her
headphones, over
the feathers of the
gnawed bird carcass
in the backyard
where I shoveled
snow in late dark
onto the blood,
bones and feathers.

And I smelled, in
youth, prophet rot
fruit below loading
dock edge heights.

And I heard the
itch in the night,
louder than a
whirlwind, softer
than a breath, a
compass-setting
off the map.

And I know she
told him: I am
your island, you
are my fortress,
neither debt nor
wealth, nor demons,
nor powers, nor

tempting, nor
weaknesses, nor
now, nor future,
nor then, nor height,
nor depth, nor width,
nor sons nor daughters,
nor two brothers
crying in their many
wildernesses, nor all,
nor nothing, shall
force us to look away.

And I heard her
tell me
black white.

And I was
shepherdless,
pastureless,
waterless,
tableless,
but armed
with the fist of
my deliverance
into and through
the valley of shadow.

And I sing:
Amen, Alleluia, Amen.

The Day Before the 1996 Democratic National Convention

They were famous and short,
the two of them and the folkie others,
guitarless, skittering and kittering
around the empty afternoon stage
like eight-year-old cousins
who see each other rarely
and make the most of it when they do.

He was that night's musical headliner,
sideshow to the pols,
who I saw out of the corner of my eye
as I headed for an interview with the ex-radical,
ex-movie star husband, ex-state senator.

She was frumpy who, that night, on stage
would be as sexy as three open blouse buttons.

Not frumpy, ordinary, washed out,
even ugly in a distinctive way
as if a saint or royalty or a blues singer.

At Target, she would have been just me or you,
on the bus, in a line for one of her concerts.

They were 46 or so, my age.

I was tall, and I never skittered.
Back in school, I would have been a hall monitor
if my school had hall monitors,
stiff as a board, walking always into the wind,
this day stiff with duty
to find and record the ex-radical,
still full of words.

They skittered and frittered
as I moved past in a hurry
on my way to somewhere backstage.

They buried my story
the next day in the paper.

Pilgrim Tale

The garbage truck, backing
down Leviticus Avenue, backed
into my big old Buick in
this slum of Visigoths and
Lombards, ignored island in
city of the blind, metropolis of
circuses and casinos. Read
the Mayor's Code and her Digest.
We violate every page. Sometimes,
we violate each other. Eunuch
Commander runs things here
although you'd think with his
power he'd enforce a different
nickname. Ingrid says he's no
eunuch. I walk past his tables of
plasticked powder and vibrant
semi-automatics and guys sweating
in May sun in Fuck Covid t-shirts,
avoid their eyes. Preacher Xavier
plays ball at the gym and
between games tells us:

> God says:
> Where were you
> when I manufactured
> the earth—
> tock, tick, tock, tick, tock, tick?
> When I dressed in clouds and fog
> the planet?
> Did you set in motion the morning?
> Do you know lightning's path?
> Can you build
> the lily?

We nod, too drained with humidity
to tell him he's full of shit, catch
our breath and run it again. Fuck
Covid. After, outside, in the night,
we walk past a small girl with a
floppy sword who spits on the brick
wall. Everyone's a critic. The debate
on the sidewalks is which is the good
thief, of the two down the corridor
from the death room. Both stole
$37.23; one killed—neither will
say—both will die. Debate moot.

You can see Preacher revving up for
another sermon, but Big Ant starts
telling us about how his father once,
when he was a little guy, stretched
him across the kitchen table and
took a knife and told him his throat
was about to be slit, but then Mrs.
Ant came in and slapped that fool
across the head and he slunk away—
she was 6'2" and 250—and Big Ant
says he's never been able to forget
the smell of pancakes burning on the
stove as he watched that thin steel
come toward him.

He complains about the dent in my
door, has to sit in back, when I
drive him to el. I tell him to shut
up. Fuck Covid. And I head up

Ecclesiastes Road and through night
with windows down and, overhead,
inert unknowable stars veiled by
incense ashes of overtime ovens
thick on the breeze.

Angels Are Out Tonight

Tonight, the typewriter keys slam rhythm
to ease coarse electricity under the skin.

The Sister of the Sacred Heart pleads alms
and sweats under her habit
as angels stride thickly east and west on her sidewalk.

Angels fly complex patterns
over the drunk anesthesiologist and the beautiful child.

Angels are out tonight.

The boy rocks his body right and left
to sleep
as angels whisper green forests in his ear
without mentioning the future gun,
a charity.

Angels are out tonight
as the fox scouts among the headstones,
as the sigh ends in stillness,
as Brother Pain is traded for Sister Death.

Tonight, angels are on the wind,
like a tune up the sidewalk,
like the white paint piers of the elevated,
like the ocean of police marching State Street,
Newman's jolly coppers, the white-glove parade.

Down the court run fast-break angels,
in the chemistry moment,
actions and reactions,
without finish or start.

Angels are out tonight,
lining the beige nursing home walls,
and planless fireflies starscape the orphan shelter lawn.

Angels with assumed names
mingle the Cubs crowd tonight after a loss
and smoke Winstons outside the gay bar
and close up shop, lowering
the commercial-grade,
roll-down,
stainless-steel security door
with a thud.

Tonight, as the handgun rusts,
angels are out,
as ballerinas pirouette the Bible verse
along the red-brick wall,
as the sacristan eats his Filet-O-Fish,
as the lawyer in her sweats
stands on the suburban balcony
overlooking an industrial park
and tries to remember
the name of the kindergarten boy who vomited.

Angels are out tonight.

Angels embrace sorrow tonight,
finding storm within the storm.

They crowd tables in the Taylor Street trattoria,
drinking water and wine and breaking bread
before the elbow macaroni arrives, parsleyed,
the last supper of the night.

Angels run a marathon tonight along Lake Shore Drive.
Wearing orange vests, they dig a ditch with loud machines.
They sing gospel songs
and blues hymns
and country & western anthems
and Ubi Caritas.

In the sanctuary, a lieutenant kneels.
Angels echo in the high church space
along the stained-glass annunciation.
My soul magnifies, she said.

Angels are out tonight.

As I walk along Clark Street
through the cold night to apologize,
angels hide in the space behind the street lights,
and my sister balances
the weight of all that has come and all that
will happen, and my mother's ashes are harmless,
and the aunt who saved my life
is willowy and curly blond still
in the backyard with the baby I was.

Latter-day angels tonight are out,
and bicoastal angels,
and special needs angels,
and glass-half-full angels,
Latin-rite angels,
strip club angels,
handyman angels,
service dog angels,
the heavenly host in mufti.

Tonight, the woman
wearing eight layers of pants and six shirts,
asleep in the tent on the Broadway sidewalk
amid metal restaurant tables and chairs
is with angels
swinging like the little girl she once was,
rising up,
swooping back,
legs building height,
and, at the top of her high, high arc,
she lets go
and flies up and out,
into the light,
the biblical furnace
where all pain is burned off like dross,
revealing pure.

At the alderman's office, the precinct captain
takes the call and dispatches a crew of angels
to fill the potholes on a short street outside the ward,
through inattention or devotion or commotion or obligation
or corruption or inspiration or sedation or kindness.

Angels are out tonight.

The Pope works as a bouncer.
The Boston Celtic drives a hack.
A poem is written on the alley wall of a downtown hotel
in pencil on sooty bricks, never to be read.
And angels stir the coffee
in every cup on every table
in the hotel's rooftop restaurant
and two miles away at the homeless refuge
and in the Mayor's kitchen

and after the banker has said the rosary
and untouched between lovers
bending toward each other
and whispering, unknowing, the secret of breathing.

Angels are out tonight.

Michael and Gabriel, Uriel and Raphael,
Jegudiel, Selaphiel, Barachiel,
the thrones and dominations,
the cherubim and seraphim,
tonight amble the glittered Andersonville pavement
and climb the shadowed Englewood apartment stairs
and sit at the edge of dark in the Glenview yard
where a man who knows he is dying
barbecues for the ones inside,
each tock and tick mundane and solemn.

Tonight, angels sleep on the Red Line
from Howard to 95th and back and back and back.

Tonight, Tri-State Tollway motorists
barrel through the I-Pass lanes,
avoiding the tollbooth angels chanting the Daily Office.

Tonight, angels fall asleep in the ice-white television light.
Angels fight on the carpet
until Mom takes the plastic baby away from them.
Angels in the hotel room
can't take their clothes off fast enough.

Angels are out tonight,
running around the university track,
each step an eternity, each exhalation another Big Bang.

In the Sovereign Tap, angels caress their Miller Lites
and watch Fred Astaire in *The Royal Wedding*
in between used car commercials.

Angels tonight await the Second Coming,
know they need,
know they want,
know they have no idea,
feel the high wearing off,
leave a backpack on the platform,
take an extra base,
twitch,
stalk,
run at the nose,
run on empty,
run to danger.

In the silence above the alleys,
angels are out tonight
as urgent rats,
worshipped in India,
revered in Rome and China and Old Japan,
jitter from hole to hole, the volted circuit.

Tonight, early drafts are put through the shredder
for no reason but delight at spaghetti-ed paper,
a dry meal of textured wonder and portent,
a gluten-free repast and echo of the halls of heaven.

Dust

She would not dust the glass tabletop
in the bedroom where he died.

It was the flakes from his skin
that had floated on the air, his dandruff,
the particles of the wretched remaining lung
expelled with tiny beads of blood
in the final coughings.

It grew thick as mold. Sunny mornings,
she sat at odd edges of the bed to see the dust
spotlighted in the rays for minutes enough.
Gloomy days, she sat in the spot,
knowing there was no secret to be revealed.

She fell once because she would not
put a restraining hand on the glass.
Her head hit the table corner,
and her light snuffed.

Later, the crew came, and the dust was watered
and wiped by a frantic cleaner on his work's first day.

On the second, he didn't appear.

About the Author

Patrick T. Reardon, a three-time nominee for a Pushcart Prize, is the author of 11 books, including the poetry collection *Requiem for David* and the history *The Loop: The "L" Tracks That Shaped and Saved Chicago*. His poetry has appeared in *Burningwood Literary Journal, Eclectica, Esthetic Apostle, Ground Fresh Thursday, Literary Orphans, Rhino, Spank the Carp, Main Street Rag, The Write Launch, Hey I'm Alive, Meat for Tea, Silver Birch Press, Tipton Poetry Journal, UCity Review,* and *Under a Warm Green Linden.* Reardon, who worked as a *Chicago Tribune* reporter for 32 years, has published freelance articles, essays, and book reviews widely in such publications as the *Tribune, Chicago Sun-Times,* the *Chicago Reader, Crain's Chicago Business, National Catholic Reporter,* and *U.S. Catholic.* His memoir in prose poems *Puddin': The Autobiography of a Baby* is forthcoming from Third World Press.

Made in the USA
Monee, IL
13 September 2022